Moleskine on a Coffee Table

by Hidden Bear

Raw Earth Ink
2021

This book is a work of poetry.

Copyright 2021 by Hidden Bear

All rights reserved. No part of this book may be reproduced or used in any manner without express written permission from the author except in the case of quotations used in a book review in which a clear link to the source of the quote and its author is required.

Second paperback edition February 2021

Cover design by tara caribou

ISBN 978-1-7360417-3-4 (paperback)

Published by Raw Earth Ink
PO Box 39332
Ninilchik, AK 99639
www.taracaribou.com

Introduction

This book is the fulfillment of a promise I made to myself. As a middle schooler, I fell in love with Emo music. The distorted guitar and high ranging vocals matched my newly discovered teenage angst perfectly, but the lyrics inspired me the most. Artists committed to one goal: Finding new ways of being sad and new ways of expressing it. At the tender age of thirteen, I truly believed I was experiencing sadness. With age, I have come to know sorrow and joy in a way my younger self did not understand. Nevertheless, this emotion I felt compelled me to create. I remember the first time I tried to write a somber hymn in the back of my study hall class. I finished and felt pride in my act of creation. That wonderful feeling was followed by a feeling of disgust as I reread my work. I have never outgrown these drastic mood swings. Whenever I finish a poem it returns to me like an old nemesis. Once my excitement settles, I write draft after draft after draft after draft. This obsessive writing process still haunts me and creates crippling hesitation with sharing my work.

I have since lost that first poem, but it began a love of writing poetry I have carried through adolescence and into adulthood. That seventh-grade dreamer used to walk through the library at school and imagine volumes of my poems and writings on the shelves. Students being forced to read my work and analyze it. And yet, shame slowly and quietly killed my dreams. I had never shared my poems before or talked to anyone about them outside of my family. And over time, one of my favorite things became a secret. One I would keep for years. In college, I discovered I could sound intellectual by quoting classic literature or poetry. I am sure I annoyed my classmates with my pretentiousness, (sorry, y'all.) But it did help create space; Space I could use to own something I loved and shed my feelings of shame. I took old poems I had kept with me, composed a few new ones, and wrote this book. I self-published the first edition and it was available for purchase for a full two weeks before I took it down. After completing the book, the hesitation returned, and I couldn't compel myself to try and market it. Then I stopped writing entirely. I had fulfilled my goal of publishing a book of poems. Poems that no one read, and no one purchased. I was still miles from achieving my naïve seventh-grade dream and I quit anyway.

And then as an adult, I had a thought: *why not keep writing?* My shame and my sense of defeat had taken away something I loved. In 2019, I launched hiddenbearpoet.com and decided to pick up this old passion once more. I am determined that the second edition of this book is just an initial contribution to a large body of work. This book is an archive of nearly 10 years of secret poems scribbled in composition books, emails to myself, and a Moleskine notebook I carried through college. It is a memorial to all the years I wrote only to myself, and to the poet I was when I began. When I read it, I see all the different versions of myself and all that happened to these other me's. Though I have changed through the years, I will always be that middle school dreamer believing he could change the world with his words.

I hope this work reminds you of all your previous selves and all they carried you through. Thanks for the support!

Hidden Bear

Dedication

To my bride, my partner, and my love,
for all your support.
To my children,
I hope I inspire you to find your own words
and use them boldly.

Section One:
Virtue
May middle school perspective help you see.

1
Empty ears and still drums
City sounds distant and silent
The Quiet stabbing your peace
Solitude feels cruel and violent

Alone you can hear yourself
Your soul's torment finally weeps
Wait in this moment as the tears flow
Let Silence give your soul release

2
Broken promises cut deeper than glass
Mending is always an option
But you must gather all the pieces
One missing piece produces toxin

Bitterness poisoning the connection
The image of your loved one twists
Leaving a caricature in place of a person
Slowly the window closes on forgiveness

3
This moment is ordinary
Take Joy because you can
Soak in the emotionlessness
Reality moving on plan

No racing heart or bad news
Just you sitting and reading a book
Glance around at your setting
Ordinary becomes your favorite nook

4
The world is filled with the selfish
Being like them is too easy a task
You are not so frail, my dear
Kindness is a heroic ask

Gentleness silences angry voices
Greed destroyed in a kind word
This is your highest calling
Selfishness in you is cured

5
You are not so weak
Have you not endured until now?
Outlasted the marathon
Keeping perseverance's Vow

You can trust the strength of your feet
This path is mysterious and may hurt
But you've survived every other path
Your legs have continued to work

6
Wait and breathe slowly
Close your eyes and rest
Calm your emotion for a minute
Release that pent up stress

Be rid of the need to rush
Productivity is not life's purpose
Take five milligrams of patience
A prescription to be less nervous

7
Creativity dies at the time clock
Counting dollars for my budget
It's never enough with each pay raise
Driving my heart to covet

Long hours and no time off
No sacrifice too great for my empire
My ears ignoring all warnings aside
And I died, alone, rich and un-retired

8
Why can't you just be like me?
Just stop being different
I don't understand you at all
I'm trying my best to be reverent

Before you were just an idea
Your life just seemed so wrong
You taught me and I learned at last
Different melodies of the same song

9
How was your day?
Do you actually know?
Have you considered it?
What is your status quo?

Reflect back on each moment
Do you have feelings you left behind?
Words you left unspoken
Replay it all and pay every mind

10
Shaken by fear and my hands sweat
I grasp my confidence and rise
I am moved to action once again
To my challenge I focus my eyes

Fear wrapping around my heart
Whispering failure into my ears
Lies! I cry as I raise my hands
To wage war on my fears

11
Will hatred defeat me?
Will my love kill me in the end?
Standing against the hate of man
No innocence I will not defend

I rest my hands on those ancient handles
I pull open the doors as dust flies
Grabbing my hope, I bow
Praying for strength and blue skies

Section Two:
Prom Night
May love make you feel like a teenager again.

Crushing

I speak with empty words
When I am with you I just feel weak
And when you smile I feel a rush
When you laugh I just feel joy
When we sit in silence together I hear you
When we hold hands I feel at home
Words articulate inadequately my feelings
My heart's twisting and flutters
Words abandon my mind; flooded with feeling

To teleport you to my muddled mind
My brain atrophied by you
While my words are caged like lions
They ought to shimmer like the belt of Orion
Yet my tongue sticks to the roof of my mouth
My heartbeat carries me as a plane heading south

I and We

Meeting, greeting, and flirting are great
Dinners, conversation, and laid back dates
Mystery around each question, each time
Checking with our friends for confirmation signs

Acting different, hiding ourselves
Putting uniqueness on the shelves
The game of masks each time
Immature feelings shiver down our spines

Yet new relationship is supplanted
And everything moves stagnant
Texts showing only "read"
Suddenly love is dead

A word more experienced than defined
Pursued or avoided; our hearts still bind
The death of "I" is found in its wake
But for the birth of we, I's life forsake

Chasing

I once sentenced myself to solitary contentment
Isolation and happiness; home I called it
In my box of calm; simplicity
A solo journey through reality
Enter the one who freed me from it all
Calling my name and my heart's stall
An awkward smile seems perfect
Ending my sentence seems worth it
Forced to wait for this revelation
Unable to move on from realization
The invasion of her presence
Yet feels like a thousand heavens
Fall from my own idealized independence
She crowned me king from among the peasants
Like a sea crashing over top of me
Thinking I'd drown; she's my safety
A new sentence imposed by cries of my heart
Not a cage but taking the stage for my part
Once happy to journey as a lone wanderer
Now I can't see a moment without her

The long night

My beloved hold on
The night is long and suffering
But morning unites us
My hand's agony in loneliness
My ears burn for your voice
But a void between us
Separated ten miles feeling like ten thousand
At school your smile weakens me
But tonight my knees buckle different
My beloved hold on
This last month of perfection but for the nights
This temporary separation aches my soul
Visions of your beauty haunt my waking dreams
I long for you and you for me
Find hope that the long day is ours
You and I share the same times
I found heaven among my living hell
Long is the night my beloved
And sixteen is a curse and parents enforce it
Forced from your tender arms
Lost in time without your hello kitty wristwatch
My beloved hold on
The night's brutality has no mercy
My only hope is the promise of your face on that bus
So my beloved hold on for soon the night will end
Hold on my beloved

Unique

Lost in a forest of butterfly wings
Tickle my hopes, risking my appetite
You splinter my focus all day
Can this love help me take flight?
Does anyone compare to this purity?
What raw emotion explodes in my chest
For what hope do others have to feel this
I know that our love unique is best

Section Three:
Vices
May we only be ensnared by our best.

Whose arms to trust if not mine

Their stares shake my soul as reality deceives
Wreathed in flame but it's really a carpet floor
The moment settles like an ancient building
Fractured visions of torment fade out of focus
Remove my knife from my back
Its deep wound filled with delusional poison

Broken trust has no reparations that can be found
Time is a cruel tormentor and healing an elusive comrade
Surrounding by truthful hands; my voice drifts beyond them
Lies, disguised
No space can comfort, no words can speak, no inspiration comes

Whose are these?
The arms of my betrayer and my savior,
The arms of my beloved and my enemy

Whose arms to trust if not my own?
My perspective pixilated
My vision like blurred polaroids
Anxiety coating the world in horror film lighting
Resemblance to flowers on a battlefield,
the petals fall but my arms cannot reach

My reductive hope slides through my fingers
If flowers hold no hope then beauty is a lie
For whose arms to trust if not my own?

My father's voice of shame shouts my failures
Humiliation as my reality is painted by a mad man
The straight arrow that turns, my blessing and poison
The snakes tongue is worse than his fangs
Piercings heal but broken hearts live forever in memory

My burden carries me awake through the nights, my eyes twitch
Weeks without sleep and a thousand nightmares
When hope seems ended the rising sun reunites me to time

Structure and schedule is a handhold for me
The warmth reminds me of deserts of fire quenched by a thousand oceans
For though my arms I cannot trust
These few arms of angels hold me steady
in the waning light

The task at hand

Every day I wake up and have my loved ones near
But what do I do for those who have no one dear?
What do I do for those paralyzed by fear?
What have I done today?

Every day I have food to eat
Every day I have friends to greet
What about those I have yet to meet?
Who don't even have shoes for their feet?
What have I done today?

What have I done for my fellowman?
Did I watch him fall or help him stand?
Have I slandered their names?
Have I played Hate's games?
What have I done today?

Is someone broken I could help?
Feel the feelings they felt?
Could I not stop to help a stranger?
Listen to that awkward suicidal teenager?
What have I done today?

Will they know me by my love?
Will I respond to their apathetic shrugs?
What have I done today?

Was I too busy caught up in life?
To comfort the widowed wife?
Did I hear the homeless on the streets?
Was I there for the prisoners, killers, and creeps?
Did I love the unlovable?
Deal with the intolerable?

What did I do today?

Shuffle

I cannot lose another dollar
One more drink to burn my throat
To remind me to forget again
Reality still eviscerates my soul
At the table and glass I heal

"That pretty lady think I'm rich"

Maybe I can lie on credit and lock my shackles
Bind me up in my golden chains
But I still owe ten percent on those
These cards always there for me
Construct my house of heart and diamond
Finish with that sweet clover shaped beauty
but I cut my finger on a spade
These four shapes of two colors free me
My false hope built up my house of cards
Soon to crash at the slightest breeze

Unlimited

There are 12 steps to fix the worlds

One: find humanity
The dark crevices of a broken heart;
Hidden in the center is the warmth of innocent start
There to heal broken bones and answer 2 year old banana phones

Two: open your ears
Listening mends the wounds that time can't
In your own silence, understanding of someone else comes
Grace is born in listening's hands

Three: let your money free
Loose your pockets from the prerequisites
Free your soul to kindness
Break your vaulted wallet and be free

Four: love
Love is not an emotion but a beautiful choice
Love for no reason other than purpose
Love all who come, for this work is eternal

Five: stand for justice
Justice exists in the efforts of exhausted people
A battlefield filled with sacrificial blood is sacred
But the blood of the innocent stains everyone's hands

Six: talk to each other
Put down your screens and cynical attitudes
Let your verbiage be heard; untyped
Let your tongue shape syllables that shape the world
Raise your glorious voice

Seven: be a neighbor
Change a tire for a stranger, pay for another's meal
Invite someone over for a BBQ on a summer afternoon
Reach across the street with arms of fellowship

Eight: read a book
Pick up that old leather bound tradition
Lose yourself in the pages of literature
Care for a fictional character and feel their emotions
Ride the adventure of imagination
For creativity is its own drug

Nine: learn a new culture
Ignorance is incomplete armor and leaves one exposed
Culture challenges your traditions and shakes your foundations
What remains can only be your roots
Respect what is different and shackle prejudice

Ten: walk ten miles
Find a stranger and grab their shoes
Put them on and walk
Footfalls are the symphony of grace
The center of a person is ten miles wide

know every inch

Eleven: find a new place
Get out of your safe and familiar
Shake the routine from your shoes
The world's wonder can fill your mind
Then your worries cannot plant their roots

Twelve: compromise
Two minds see blurry but four see clearly
Compromise is the laces of society
Blurred people unite to reveal clear brilliant images
Lay down your right-ness for each other
In the end people matter most

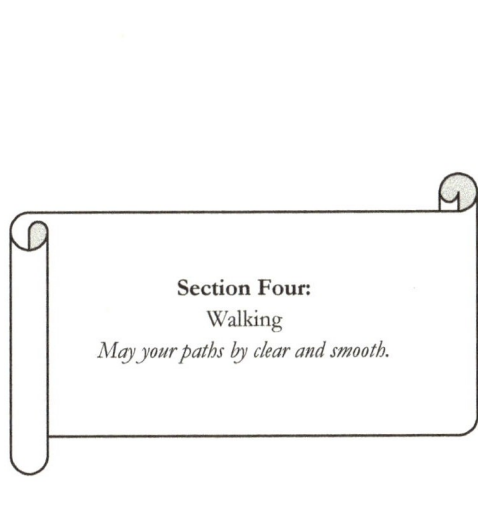

Section Four:
Walking
May your paths by clear and smooth.

Pathways

My feet have a short memory
Forgetting where to go and where they've been
Roads traveled with shuffling thoughts
I cannot rely on their memory

They travel left and right but lose their way
Neon signs and flashing lights quickly reroute
Rushing to comfort; leaving the road
Evaporating opportunity left in their wanderings

My feet have short memory
Their longing for miles aches my toes, the heels unworn
sit in want
My shoes checked-in at the door
Lying unused on the floor abandoned
For my feet find themselves and rarely return
Every landscape holds marks of my print
Yet my destination is elusive

My feet have a short memory
Aimlessness fills my days
My feet find a compass
North guides hopes
South my dreams
West my pains
And East my clear direction

Pulled by magnetism to opposing orientations
Pulling my feet off any road to be lost again
The vast open oceans of indecisive life
Leaving beautiful sunsets and fruitless trees

The compass arrow swirling
Maps shifting as the land grows dark
The twisting forests encircle my feet,
Vines snap from the force of my walk
The forest bows to my stomping,
though my hands remain tied and my mouth taped shut

My feet have a short memory
Darkness fought by the rays of a cresting sunrise
Hope springs and flows in a stream
Swirling around my ankles and my feet stir

Amidst the whirlpool my toes long for pathway
Focused my feet see among the shrubs a faint curved path
Cuts the forest
Walking the path my feet are content
But behold my feet soon wander off to adventures glory

My feet have a short memory

Above

My elevator goes sideways
It can pass through walls and shatter vaults
My elevator can go to any floor on any street
It flows through the farms, villages, and cities
From its safety I watch empires fall and collapse
I can steal money and rescue children
I feed the homeless and attack criminals
All from my elevator

I correct mistakes and see further than everyone
I can outrun anything and take all I wish
My elevator takes me, it has no limits
My elevator can fight a war and make a phone call
My feet stay planted as the world swirls past
I fear nothing in my elevator for who can reach me?

In my elevator I have it all.

Through another's eyes

I seek to find safety
Yet none permit it
Corruption is my oppressor
Pollution my oxygen
Every toxic breath strangles me
Rotten food satiates my hunger
Stand near trees just to breathe
That oxygen purifies my blood
I cannot walk upright
The weight of oppression
Breaks my ankles and I lose my boots
The streets arms open and take me in
Just another alleyway ornament

Argument

I speak and my words are storming oceans
You clash with storms of lightning
Despite my best I can't calm either
And so we destroy each other and create silence
I would have that you and I speak.
Speak calmed words, of kindness and love
Can you not remember the one you loved?
Or is it me that has forgotten you?
I walk a mile in your shoes
You walk a mile in mine
But now we are just two miles apart
Heart tearing at the seams by each other's hands
Our eyes reflect hidden words
And our hands drift apart
The calm returns
But only when I am alone

Alleyways

White pillars and dark shadows
I see your lips are polished clean after you speak
The white steeple; the pinnacle of power
And the people starve in alleyways

Your selfishness is as unlimited as your waistline
Corrupt appetites cannot be satisfied
And the people starve in alleyways

You pick fights like children in a playground
Diamond rings and coats soaked in your people's tears
Your breath smells of liquor and lies
Everything under your control yet we take no more
And the people starve in alleyways

Foolish old men filled with pride
My eye turns to the districts
Law and order except for us holy few
Private jets reach the heights
War looks like art from that distance
And the people starve in alleyways

Courage

I only fear four things

ONE:
Untied shoelaces bring me terror
It's just not safe
Their lifeless bodies flail about
Crushed under a careless master
Neglect poisoning our souls
Also you might trip

TWO:
Holes in a bounce house
The collapsing heavy rubber
It suffocates all it touches
Money spent on death
Collecting germs of bacteria on each surface
Children's laughter covering the sound of pain
Abuse repeating like bounces in that house
Of these things I am truly afraid
Also someone could get hurt

THREE:
Insects with wings are my nightmare
I cannot imagine a time I wasn't gripped with fear
That buzz of flapping wings shakes me
I tremble at their superiority
They change with the winds of power
Bending to the winds of self interests

They come to exploit me
Also they have diseases

FOUR:
Corruption taking its place in my heart
Black tar covering my soul
Straining to breathe through it
Integrity crumbles into the oiled oceans
I fear this over any charge leveled at me:
That I sold myself
Also it makes it hard to get anything done.

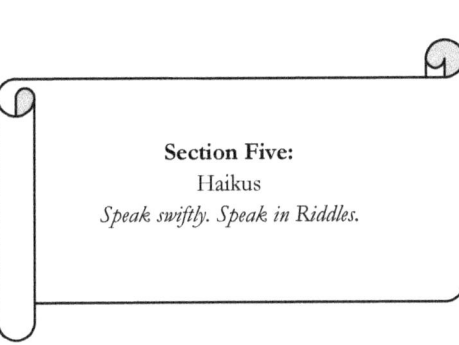

Section Five:
Haikus
Speak swiftly. Speak in Riddles.

Control

You do not choose birth
Yet it happens despite you
Death will be the same

Work

Find a soft couch now
The working man has no rest
But his family eats

Chairs

Stacking hope like chairs
Stored in the corner all alone
Until life seats you

Fly

Raise your golden wings
Stretch them to the sky once more
Rise up new standard

Royalty

Age separates us
Do not fear your own aging
It is a silver crown

Freedom

Your monster is awake
Only you can give it rest
Forgiveness frees you

Light

The light still guides you
Though you have forgotten it
It shines on you still

A Final Note

You did it. Here we are on the final page. I hope this work stirred something in your heart. I hope these words reminded you of someone you used to be. I hope that motivates you to become the best version of yourself. I hope my voice in your life has produced something good, or if nothing else gave you a break from the pain you are facing. I can't tell you what incredible joy I feel knowing that over a decade of shifting emotions, hesitation, and scribbled words has led us here, to the last page of my book. I just wanted to say thank you again for supporting me and being a part of my dream.

All the best,

HB

www.ingramcontent.com/pod-product-compliance
Lightning Source LLC
Chambersburg PA
CBHW031308060426
42444CB00032B/795